LITTLE

LAW

BOOKS

LITTLE

LAW

BOOKS

M.H. Hoeflich & John Moreland

TALBOT
PUBLISHING
Clark, New Jersey
2025

TALBOT PUBLISHING

AN IMPRINT OF

THE LAWBOOK EXCHANGE, LTD.
33 Terminal Avenue
Clark, New Jersey 07066-1321

Please see our website for a selection of our other publications and fine facsimile reprints of classic works of legal history:
www.lawbookexchange.com

For my deceased puppy, Poogli.
M.H. HOEFLICH

I MAGINE, if you will, arriving at the gates of Heaven and being ushered into paradise. You are offered a guided tour of the celestial realm and asked what you would especially like to see. If you are legal bibliophiles, as we are, you will first ask where the libraries and bookshops are located. In such Heavenly bookish sites, you will find—or so you hope—miles of shelves filled with every law book ever published (all signed by the authors, of course). But even in Heaven, books need to be ordered and arranged and, therefore, these celestial law books will have been arranged by the Heavenly Law Librarian (Morris Cohen, naturally)[1] in categories based upon subject and special attributes. In a far corner, you will find a special section, designated "Little Law Books." In this brief piece, we provide a small preview of this rather unusual law book format.

Although law books, both printed and manuscript, have been produced in a variety of sizes, formats, and bindings over the centuries, the vast majority of modern law books tend to be utilitarian, designed to serve the professional needs of their users. While there have been and continue to be a few collectors

---

[1] One of the foremost law librarians and legal bibliographers of the late 20th century, Morris L. Cohen directed the law libraries at Yale Law School and Harvard Law School. His landmark work was the six-volume *Bibliography of Early American Law* (1998), which provides readers the ability to find any American law book prior to 1860. *Yale Law School Mourns the Death of Professor and Librarian Emeritus Morris L. Cohen*, 32 YALE L. REP. 33 (2011), https://ylr. law.yale.edu/pdfs/v58-2/S11.Cohen.pdf

of law books, they tend to be far more interested in the books as examples of the historical and intellectual development of law, rather than in the books as artifacts.[2] However, certain genres of law books, e.g. those in small formats (12mo and smaller), are of historical and bibliographical significance in understanding the law book trade and the use of law books. And a few law books deserve attention purely as artifacts, as they sometimes rise to the unusual and, at times, the eccentric. These can be macabre, such as the books bound in the skins of executed criminals.[3] Or, they can be simply curious, such as some of the miniature law books which are the subject of this brief piece.

At the outset it is useful to clarify that we have deliberately chosen to use the inexact phrase "little law book" rather than the phrase "miniature book" popular with collectors.[4] There is no agreed-upon or established definition of a miniature book, even among bibliographers. One generally states that any book that is smaller than three inches by five inches is a miniature book. John Carter's reference work *ABC for Book Collectors* states that "[a]ny volume below 2" x 1 ½" would probably qualify [as a miniature book]."[5] Another authority states that a book in 64mo, in which each section of the book consists of a single printed page with sixty-four text pages, would qualify, while others simply say that every collector and bibliographer has his or her own definition.[6] By using "little" rather than "miniature," we hope that we may escape such bibliographical quibbles and, instead, focus on law

---

2 M.H. Hoeflich, *Legal History and the History of the Book: Variations on a Theme*, 46 U. Kansas L. Rev. 416 (1998).

3 Megan Rosenbloom, Dark Archives: A Librarian's Investigation into the Science and History of Books Bound in Human Skin 95 (2021).

4 *See* Patricia Pistner & Jan Storm van Leeuwen Pistner, Matter of Size: Miniature Bindings & Texts From the Collection of Patricia J. Pistner (2019).

5 John Carter, ABC For Book Collectors 169 (9th ed. 2016).

6 *Book Formats*, Antiquarian Booksellers' Assoc. of Am., Glossary of Terms, https://www.abaa.org/glossary/entry/book-formats

books that are diminutive in size (normally 32mo or smaller) and the unusual aspects of this format. Interestingly, the three standard studies of miniature books do not discuss law books at all.[7] This piece, in part, is designed to fill that scholarly void.

There is no question that the predominant formats for Anglo-American law books from the fifteenth century through the twentieth century were folio and quarto. Smaller formats existed, as we will discuss, but were not as common— with the exception of civil and canon law books. These were often produced in pocket size, especially elementary texts such as Justinian's *Institutes* or even sections of the *Corpus Juris Civilis*. Certainly, these civil law texts and commentaries in small format were not produced for their aesthetic qualities, although some are rather elegantly bound. Rather, the small format must derive from the desire to produce a book that could be conveniently carried in a coat pocket or satchel to be available for easy reference and use. These were working books, not curiosities. The type was readable, if small, and margins were often of sufficient size for some annotation.[8]

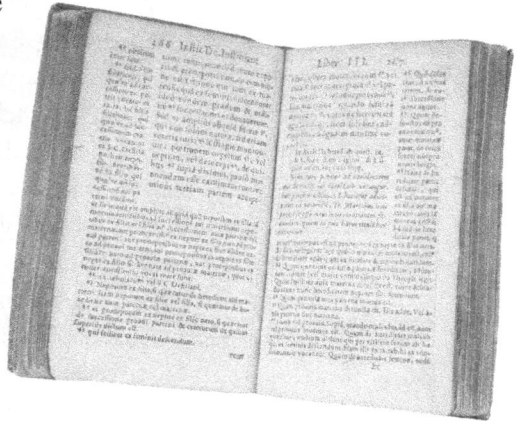

WORKING BOOKS

When we refer to "working books," we intend to signify those books whose primary purpose for the owner/reader is to

---

7 LOUIS W. BONDY, MINIATURE BOOKS: THEIR HISTORY FROM THE BEGINNINGS TO THE PRESENT DAY (1981); DORIS V. WELSH, THE HISTORY OF MINIATURE BOOKS (1987); and A. BROMER & J. EDISON, MINIATURE BOOKS: 4,000 YEARS OF TINY TREASURES (2007).

8 John D. Berry, *The Typography of Books*, TYPOFONDERIE, https://typofonderie. com/gazette/the-typography-of-books/

provide a text that can assist them in their work, whether as a lawyer, law student, government clerk, or merchant. Thus, a book which a lawyer possesses that is intended to be useful for the practice of law would be a working book. Similarly, a book intended to provide important legal information or useful forms and templates to a farmer, merchant, or mechanic would fall within the category of working books. Volumes intended to be used by those studying the law we would also include in this category, although some might include them in the "educational or children's book" category as well. We deliberately exclude what we would call "children's books" from the working book category and include these in their own category, but limit this category to books intended for grades K-12.

For the most part, little law books did not fulfill one function that larger format books did. Long rows of folios or quartos on a shelf proclaimed the owner to be a man of learning and substance.[9] Small-format books lacked this aesthetic quality, but were, undoubtedly, practical.

Lawyers throughout the past millennia have been travelers. Lawyers and judges often were required to travel under uncomfortable circumstances on horseback or in coaches and wagons.[10] To carry large, heavy law books would have been difficult or impossible. Whether carried by a Carolingian royal official in the ninth century or a territorial judge riding circuit in the nineteenth, small-format law books were extremely helpful.[11]

A useful example of a small-format civil law book is the 1751 edition of the *Enchiridion Iuris Utriusque* by Bartholomaeus Cartagena.[12] The copy in the Hoeflich collection is bound in

---

9 M.H. Hoeflich and John L. Moreland, *A 19th Century Lawyer's Life in Portraits*, 28 THE GREEN BAG 106 (2024).

10 Michael G. Chiorazzi, *Francois-Xavier Martin: Printer, Lawyer, Jurist*, 7 DUKE L. MAG. 5 (1989).

11 LAWRENCE M. FRIEDMAN, A HISTORY OF AMERICAN LAW 111-112 (4th ed. 2001).

12 BARTHOLOMAEUS CARTEGENA, ENCHIRIDION JURIS UTRIUSQUE: SEU

vellum (now quite soiled from age and use) and has several blank leaves at the end. It has a reasonably sized typeface suitable for everyday use, but the margins are so narrow that marginal annotation would not have been possible. The paper on which it is printed is quite sturdy, as witnessed by its survival over the centuries.

This volume was a working book. It was small enough to be easily carried. It is printed on good, reasonably heavy paper that would have stood up to frequent use. It is divided into two sections: canon law and civil law. Each of the sections is subdivided into titles and subjects. It is not an aesthetically pleasing book by any means, but it would have been an excellent abbreviated guide to key canon and civil law rules, perfect as an aide-memoire for a law student or a young J.U.D.[13] It was far more an outline guide than a substantive treatise that might require marginalia. The small margins making annotation difficult were probably not an issue since the text itself was a reference text rather than a primary source.

Basic working books in this small format are also found amongst common law books, although the smallest of these tend to be a bit larger, usually in 12mo or 16mo, measuring more than 3 x 5 inches in size.[14] One example is *The Young Clerk's Vade Mecum or Compleat English Law Tutor*, printed in London and reprinted at Belfast by Francis Joy in 1742. It is a compilation of precedents in a wide variety of subject areas that would have been extremely

---

DEFINITIONES, DISTINCTIONES, ET QUAESTIONES CLARE ET BREVITER DEFINITAE IURIS CANONICI ET CIVILIS: SYNOPSI BIFARIÂ, & IN PRIORE QUIDEM OMNES DECRETALIUM, AUTH. BARTHOL. À CARTHAGENA; IN POSTERIORE VERÒ OMNES INSTITUTIONUM IMPERIALIUM. AUCTORE B.S. LIBROS AC TITULOS BREVITER AC PERSPICUE EXPLANANTES AC ENUCLEANTES (Frankfurt, Joan. Frid. Fleischerum 1751).

13 *Juris utriusque doctor*, i.e. a doctorate holder in both canon and civil law.

14 A. BROMER & J. EDISON, MINIATURE BOOKS: 4,000 YEARS OF TINY TREASURES (2007). *See also* R.C. BRADBURY, ANTIQUE UNITED STATES MINIATURE BOOKS, 1690-1900 (2001).

useful to a solicitor or law clerk called upon to draft documents. Its small format, again, would have made it simple to carry to a client's residence or business, or to keep on a desk for frequent use. This particular copy was printed on cheap paper in small but readable type, and would have likely been far less costly than a larger folio or quarto volume. It was not an unusual book, but, rather, of a common type sold to the profession and to legally minded merchants.

Such small-format volumes designed for easy portability and low cost were also found throughout the United States. Two texts are worth mentioning as illustrations. The first examples are the many editions of the self-help manuals which carry titles such as *Everyman His Own Lawyer* or a close variation thereof.[15] This genre of book is quite significant both historically and bibliographically. The genre originated in England and was designed primarily for merchants, farmers, and businessmen who had need of a basic general law text with some precedents.[16] These books soon spread to the United States where they required modification for American audiences.[17] They were

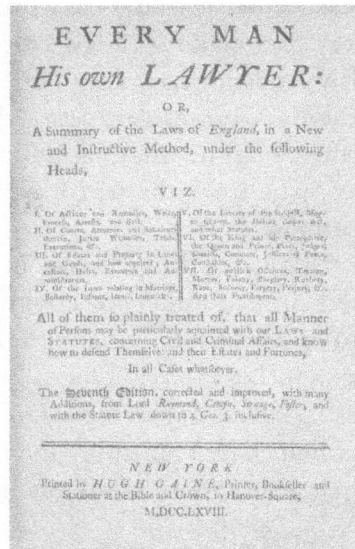

---

15 GILES JACOB, EVERY MAN HIS OWN LAWYER: OR, A SUMMARY OF THE LAWS OF ENGLAND (London, E. and R. Nutt, and R. Gosling 1736); JOHN GIFFORD, THE COMPLETE ENGLISH LAWYER; OR, EVERY MAN HIS OWN LAWYER (London, D. Jaques 1810).

16 T. WILLIAM, EVERYMAN HIS OWN LAWYER; OR, COMPLETE LAW LIBRARY (London, Sherwood, Neely and Jones 1812).

17 GILES JACOB, EVERY MAN HIS OWN LAWYER: OR, A SUMMARY OF THE LAWS OF ENGLAND, IN A NEW AND INSTRUCTIVE METHOD (New York, Hugh Gaine 1768).

printed throughout the early Republic, often edited by local lawyers and, on occasion, directed to specific professions including farmers and merchant clerks.[18] They tended to be of small format, designed for ready reference and frequent use— one can easily imagine copies sitting on merchants' desks or on bookshelves in a shop or factory or farmstead.

These volumes were rarely published by specialist law booksellers. Instead, they tended to be local productions of job printers, the type of cheap, easily saleable books, like religious primers or schoolbooks, that a job printer could produce cheaply and sell at a profit. These were often texts without copyright protection, so they could be reprinted easily.[19] Additionally, since they were commonly intended for local audiences, the audience for them would not have financially justified a national publisher's attention. They were, in effect, law books intended to stay within the state where they were printed.

Because they contained model documents and precedents, the local nature of these volumes was extremely important. A merchant in Philadelphia would find a New York volume based on New York law of limited utility. To the legal historian, then, they provide an important source for understanding the local variations in private law and emphasize the distinct differences between the states. For any given state, they paint a concise picture

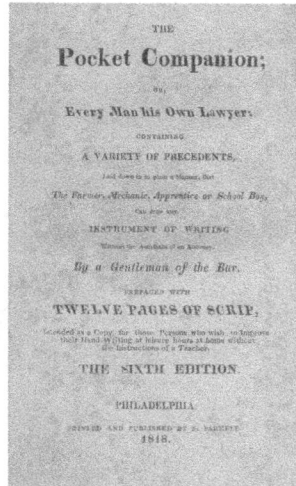

---

18 THE POCKET COMPANION; OR, EVERY MAN HIS OWN LAWYER; BY A GENTLEMAN OF THE BAR; LAID DOWN IN SO PLAIN A MANNER, THAT THE FARMER, MECHANIC, APPRENTICE, OR SCHOOL BOY, CAN DRAW ANY INSTRUMENT OF WRITING, WITHOUT THE ASSISTANCE OF AN ATTORNEY (Philadelphia, M'Carty & Davis 1819).

19 James M. Wells, *American Printing: The Search for Self-Sufficiency*, AM. ANTIQUARIAN SOC. 294 (1984).

of general law knowledge amongst the mercantile population, the subjects that were of most importance to the average clerk or merchant classes, and the forms of documents most crucial for merchants, farmers, and other users who purchased these books.

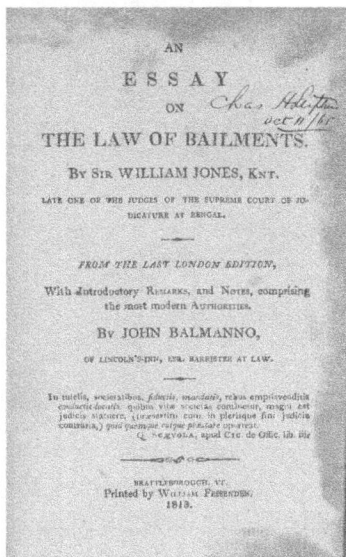

The second text, which is of interest because it was issued both as a "little law book" and in a more ordinary, larger format, is Sir William Jones' classic *An Essay on the Law of Bailments*, first published at London in 1781.[20] It is a short, heavily documented volume. Despite its brevity, it became popular almost immediately because it deals with a subject of intense interest amongst lawyers. The law of bailments was especially essential to eighteenth and nineteenth-century business and mercantile transactions. That Joseph Story chose to write a treatise on the subject (dependent upon Jones' text) several decades later testifies to this.[21]

Jones' treatise was often reprinted in the United States beginning in the late eighteenth century, and became one of the most frequently reprinted legal treatises in the United States during the early republic.[22] These volumes were almost always of small format, a fact which is interesting but not necessarily surprising. In part, one may speculate that the size of the treatise

20 WILLIAM JONES, AN ESSAY ON THE LAW OF BAILMENTS (London, J. Nichols 1781).

21 JOSEPH STORY, COMMENTARIES ON THE LAW OF BAILMENTS (Cambridge, Hilliard and Brown 1832).

22 Sir William Jones (1746-1794) IN THOMAS A. SEBEOK, PORTRAITS OF LINGUISTS: A BIOGRAPHICAL SOURCE BOOK FOR THE HISTORY OF WESTERN LINGUISTICS, 1746-1963 (1966).

itself, quite short, lent itself to a small format which would avoid the problem of a larger format book being extremely thin and, as a result, rather flimsy, like a pamphlet. But there are other possibilities as well.

Were small-format law books necessarily less expensive than larger format books? The printing process itself gives us some hints. Most of these volumes were not printed and published by the large specialist booksellers in Eastern urban cities. They were printed by newspaper and job printers in smaller towns.[23] These printers would have been using standard hand presses and would have most likely been used to standard-sized paper that would fit on a jobber's press.[24] It is difficult to know whether they were sold already bound. Cloth bindings were not available before 1820.[25] So, books would either be sold in sheets, cheap temporary paper bindings, or in inexpensive leather. Presumably, smaller pieces of leather would have been cheaper, so size of the volume would have had some impact on pricing. Often buyers would have their books bound themselves, so the cost of binding would not have figured into the price of the book from the bookseller.

What would have significantly affected the price, however, was the number of sheets required to print a book.[26] Smaller pages and smaller type used printing paper more efficiently and could, in fact, significantly lower the cost of the finished book. This is quite clearly pointed out in a report of a Congressional committee on public printing which examined the ways in which some printers lowered their costs and increased their profits significantly by

---

23 Chiorazzi, *supra* note 10, at 7.

24 PARKE ROUSE, THE PRINTER IN EIGHTEENTH-CENTURY WILLIAMSBURG 21 (2019).

25 Paul W. Nash, *Two Hundred Years of Publisher's Cloth*, 1 J PRINTING HIST. SOC. 241 (2024).

26 Iiro Tiihonen, Leo Lahti & Mikko Tolonen, *Print Culture and Economic Constraints: A Quantitative Analysis of Book Prices in Eighteenth-Century Britain*, 94 EXPLORATIONS IN ECON. HIST. 7 (2024).

reducing the size of text and type in government publications.[27] Certainly, evidence from antebellum law booksellers' catalogues suggests that copies of Jones' volume were quite inexpensive, averaging between $1.50 and 2.00 regardless of date or editor.[28]

Small-format working law books were an important part of the nineteenth-century law book market because they offered convenient, easy to carry, inexpensive manuals for lawyers, law students, and merchants with an interest in the law. They helped to spread both basic common law rules and essential forms to a large number of interested readers. They did not require either the space or investment that larger-format reports, digests, or treatises demanded. Indeed, we may well speculate that most of these small-format books were of far greater importance to non-lawyers and law students than to established lawyers, who needed far more comprehensive and sophisticated sources. In many cases, these were the volumes of "law for the common man."[29] Their texts provide law and book historians a view of a small but significant source of revenue for local job printers who were constantly seeking printing business, were it religious manuals, newspapers, broadsides, or educational manuals.

SOME SPECIALIST WORKING LAW BOOKS

As Sanford Levinson and other scholars have observed, the Constitution of the United States is more than a constitutive legal text.[30] It is, in fact, a secular holy book for vast numbers

---

27 U.S. TEL.--EXTRA, June 28, 1828 at 240-243.

28 *See, e.g.*, TOPLIFF JOHNSON, J. WARNER JOHNSON & S.P. PUTNAM, JOHNSONS' LAW CATALOGUE 67 (Philadelphia, 1850), WILLIAM JONES, ESSAY ON THE LAW OF BAILMENTS (Philadelphia, 1836)- $2.00; CHARLES C. LITTLE, JAMES P. BROWN & AUGUSTUS FLAGG, GENERAL CATALOGUE OF LAW BOOKS 74 (Boston, 1856), WILLIAM JONES, ESSAY ON THE LAW OF BAILMENTS (Philadelphia, 1836)-$2.00.

29 FRIEDMAN, *supra* note 11, at 313.

30 *See* SANFORD LEVINSON, CONSTITUTIONAL FAITH (2011).

of Americans. Thus, it is not at all surprising that we find that the Constitution has been reprinted in multiple formats over its history, including that of a "little law book."

In the antebellum period, copies of the U.S. Constitution were often—if not most frequently—printed with other texts such as the texts of state constitutions, the Declaration of Independence, or other legal and political documents.[31] These tended to be in smaller formats, particularly octavo, so they would have been convenient to be carried in a pocket or purse.

In the late twentieth and early twenty-first century, even smaller copies of the Constitution have become popular for many readers to carry in their pockets, often to be pulled out to demonstrate their loyalty to the text of the document and in support for the Originalist approach to constitutional interpretation.[32] This is more of a political statement, and of symbolic utility rather than the practical necessity of a working lawyer or law student. In the case of these small volume texts, format is important for maximum exposure. The fact that they are not printed by law book publishers is irrelevant since they are intended for free distribution rather than sale.[33]

The other categories of small, law-related working book one finds commonly in the nineteenth and early twentieth century are rules of court and pocket diaries designed for lawyers' use.[34] Both were designed to be carried in a lawyer's pocket. They

---

31 Emily Sneff, *With the Declaration of Independence*, HARVARD GRADUATE SCH. EDUC.: DECLARATION RES. PROJECT (Oct. 4, 2016), https://declaration. fas.harvard.edu/blog/october-context

32 Even the U.S. Government Publishing Office sells pocket Constitutions, printed under the direction of the Joint Committee on Printing. *The Constitution of the United States and the Declaration of Independence* (Pocket Edition) (2019 printing).

33 Nicholas B. Shrum, *Materializing Faith and Politics: The Unseen Power of the NCCS Pocket Constitution in American Religion*, 57 DIALOGUE 42-43 (2024).

34 M.H. Hoeflich, *Lawyers' Everyday Lives in Bygone Diaries: Durably Ephemeral Perspectives on the Day-to-Day of 19th-Century American Lawyers*, 24 GREEN BAG 311 (2021).

needed to be inexpensive, lightweight, and on paper that could be written on. One example of a book of local court rules, *Rules of the Circuits of Common Pleas, Orphans' Court, and Quarter Sessions within the 15th Judicial District of Pennsylvania* (1830), not only displays all of these characteristics, but also is bound in a rather attractive marble paper binding which would have ensured that it was visible and less likely to be lost or left behind by a busy lawyer. Lawyers' pocket diaries were also bound in inexpensive leather, as was the case with pocket diaries designed for general use. This type of binding was more practical for a volume that would see constant use.

CHILDREN'S & SCHOOL BOOKS

Children's books and schoolbooks presented special requirements for both publishers and printers. First, they had to be inexpensive in virtually all cases. These were volumes that would see hard use, even abuse, by their readers. Ideally, they would be strong enough to survive multiple uses by young children. Second, they would need to be portable, since they would be transported between home and school and, in school, between classrooms and readers. Third, a smaller format better suited small hands.

The quality of paper would also be of some importance, but judging by most nineteenth-century children's and schoolbooks, this was not a priority. The production qualities of such books were not high, and the paper and type were often of low quality.[35] Given the cost and scarcity of paper in antebellum America, it seems reasonable to speculate that better paper was reserved for more expensive publications and correspondence sheets. In many volumes that we have examined, the paper used seems very much like that used for newspapers. Generally, these volumes were not hardbound but had paper or thin boards as covers.

---

35 *See* University of Pittsburgh Digital Collections, *19th Century Schoolbooks*, https://digital.library.pitt.edu/collection/19th-century-schoolbooks

From a printer's and publisher's perspective, the production of law-related children's books was quite attractive. They were cheap to produce, had a large market, and would need to be frequently replaced, an early example of planned obsolescence. Unlike many children's books of the antebellum period, these books rarely had the illustrations so common to religious or story books, making them even less costly to produce.

Although these religious or story books, along with school readers, made up the vast majority of nineteenth-century children's books, it was not uncommon to find books on law and government among those printed for the children's market. The teaching of what we may broadly call "civics," including law, was a core concern of nineteenth-century primary education. Law was understood to be a critical part of every literate person's educational foundation, for only by understanding the law could one be a fully participating member of the citizenry.

The late, great librarian, scholar, and bibliophile Morris Cohen assembled a superb collection of children's books relating to the law. Many of these volumes, as listed and illustrated in *Law & Order Made Amusing*, a catalogue of selections from his collection displayed by the Boston College Law Library in 2019, are of small format and fit the bibliographical parameters described.[36]

One example of these law-related children's books is *Pinnock's Catechism of British Law*, published by G. and W.B. Whittaker in London in 1823.[37] George Whittaker, one of the leading book publishers of his time, was the publisher of a large series of children's books known as "Pinnock's Catechisms":

> A former teacher turned bookseller/publisher, William Pinnock (1782-1843) issued a series of "catechisms" covering a wide range of secular

---

36 KAREN BECK ET AL., LAW & ORDER MADE AMUSING: A SELECTION OF LAW BOOKS FOR CHILDREN FROM THE COLLECTION OF MORRIS L. COHEN (1998).

37 WILLIAM PINNOCK, PINNOCK'S CATECHISM OF BRITISH LAW: CONTAINING CORRECT IDEAS OF OUR CONSTITUTIONAL RIGHTS AND LIBERTIES (London, G. & W.B. Whittaker 1823).

topics in the question-and-answer format originally used for religious instruction. It is not clear who actually wrote most of these cheaply produced pamphlets, aimed at a fast-expanding non-elite juvenile market. "British Law" is. a misnomer, although the text on display surveys Britain's main institutions of government as well as English common law. [38]

The preface to the volume expresses its purpose:

> A general knowledge of the Laws and Institutions of our native country is so essentially necessary to everyone who pretends to a liberal education, that no apology seems necessary for ushering into the world the following little elementary treatise: the chief object being to present to youth a regular and systematic view of that beautiful edifice, the British Constitution—the solidity and exquisite proportions of which will be more admired and valued, the more nicely they are examined.
>
> The author has endeavored to unite brevity with clearness, in his description of rights and remedies; and as his former little treatises have met with a considerable degree of favor from an indulgent public, he feels the less diffidence in sending forth another production of his leisure hours to meet its censure or applause.[39]

The volume itself is a seventy-four page abridgement: a much-simplified version of Blackstone's *Commentaries*, perfect for a young country gentleman to prepare himself for a life as justice of the peace or magistrate.

---

38 Wilfrid Prest & Michael Widener, 250 years of Blackstone's Commentaries: An Exhibition 17 (2015).

39 Pinnock, *supra* note 37, at 2.

ESOTERICA & CURIOSA

The final major category of small-format law books which we will briefly discuss in this essay is what we refer to as "esoterica."[40] There are collectors of miniature books who collect them for their rarity and aesthetics. The range of subjects covered by these is enormous and law is one of the topics covered, although not so often as literature, biography, or religion.

In many cases, miniature law-related books were published as curiosities and the format itself was designed to appeal to the collector sensibility or to stress the eccentricity of the text. One example of such a volume is the 1836 edition of *The Code of 1650, Being a Compilation of the Earliest Laws and Orders of the General Court of Connecticut...*, a wonderfully odd volume of amusing, strange and outdated laws designed for entertainment rather than for practical use.[41] The 1836 volume has a primitive engraving at the front illustrating colonial enforcement of tobacco laws. The volume which we examine is bound in cardboard and the paper used for the text is of low quality. All of this made the book inexpensive enough to be affordable for entertainment purposes alone.

The second illustration we cite is an extremely odd volume, issued in wrappers and published in 1923 by St. Dominic's Press in the English village of Ditchling, Sussex.[42] The volume is

---

40 The American Library Association Glossary of Library and Information Science defines 'esoterica' as "Printed materials that are unusual, obscure, or specialized in nature, often collected for their rarity or uniqueness rather than their content alone." MICHAEL LEVINE-CLARK ET AL., ALA GLOSSARY OF LIBRARY AND INFORMATION SCIENCE (4th ed. 2013).

41 SILAS ANDRUS, THE CODE OF 650, BEING A COMPILATION OF THE EARLIEST LAWS AND ORDERS OF THE GENERAL COURT OF CONNECTICUT: ALSO THE CONSTITUTION, OR CIVIL COMPACT, ENTERED INTO AND ADOPTED BY THE TOWNS OF WINDSOR, HARTFORD, AND WETHERSFIELD (Hartford, Judd, Loomis & Co. 1836).

42 HILARY DOUGLAS C. PEPLAR, THE LAW THE LAWYERS KNOW ABOUT (1923).

titled *The Law the Lawyers Know About*. The author of the text
was H.D.C. Peplar, a poet.[43] A few lines from the text make its
audience clear:

> THE law the lawyers know about
> Is property and land;
> But why the leaves are on the trees,
> And why the winds disturb the seas,
> Why honey is the food of bees,
> Why horses have such tender knees,
> Why winters come and rivers freeze,
> Why faith is more than what one sees,
> And hope survives the worst disease,
> And charity is more than these,
> They do not understand.[44]

Perhaps the most interesting
aspect of the volume is that the
illustrator was Eric Gill, once a
highly popular English illustrator
who has lost public favor today.[45]
Obviously, the book's appeal lay in
the illustrations and the verse, which
were designed for enlightenment,
not instruction.

43 *Ibid.*

44 *Ibid.* at 2.

45 *Eric Gill*, NATIONAL PORTRAIT GALLERY, https://www.npg.org.uk/
collections/search/person/mp01776/eric-gill

AND LAST BUT NOT LEAST...
LITTLE BLUE BOOKS

Perhaps the most famous small-format law books published in the twentieth century were a series published by Emanuel Haldeman-Julius, a journalist, marketer, capitalist, and socialist publisher in Girard, Kansas from 1919-1978.[46] All told, Haldeman-Julius published several thousand titles on every subject he thought the public would buy, specializing in self-help, sex, history, and abridgements of literature. The Little Blue Books were published in a 3" by 5" format and tended to be either 32 or 64 pages long.[47]

A number of the self-help books were on legal subjects and the press also published a number of works by or about Clarence Darrow, who maintained a long-term relationship with Mrs. Haldeman-Julius.[48] Today, a number of collectors focus on the Little Blue Books, but they are far less well known than they were one hundred years ago.[49]

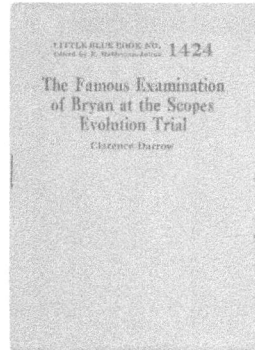

---

46 M.H. Hoeflich, *Emanuel and Marcet Haldeman-Julius: An Innovative Partnership in Publishing, in* JOHN BROWN TO BOB DOLE: MOVERS AND SHAKERS IN KANSAS HISTORY 193-204 (Virgil W. Dean ed., 1996); E. HALDEMAN-JULIUS, THE WORLD OF HALDEMAN-JULIUS (1960).

47 R.C. Johnson & T. Tanselle, *The Haldeman-Julius "Little Blue Books" as a Biographical Problem*, 64 PAPERS BIB. SOC'Y AM. 29 (1970); E. HALDEMAN-JULIUS, THE FIRST HUNDRED MILLION (1928).

48 *See* Hoeflich, *supra* note 46; M.H. Hoeflich, *Clarence Darrow and His Ties to Kansas*, 57 U. KAN. L. REV. 1177-1198 (2009).

49 The authors are currently writing a follow-up to this chapbook tentatively

FINAL REFLECTIONS

Books have backstories. The text may well be the most important element of a book, but it is certainly not the only one. Format, paper, binding, type, illustration—all of these elements have much to teach us as well. As rare book librarian Joel Silver reminds us, "contact with rare books touch[es] the spirit in ways that the law library's other holdings cannot."[50] By reaching into the past and connecting with the physical attributes of little law books, we can see the historical foundations of both civic life in early America and of the practicalities faced by the legal profession.

Happy Holidays 2025

titled "A Socialist Law Book Publisher in Southeastern Kansas: The Haldeman-Julius Little Blue Books."

50 Joel Silver, *The Role of Rare Books in Law Libraries*, 20 LEGAL REFERENCE SERVS. Q., nos. 1-2, 2001, at 85.

ILLUSTRATIONS

p. 9 – JUSTINIAN I, INSTITUTIONUM SIVE ELEMENTORUM PER TRIBUNIANUM VIRUM MAGNIFICUM MAGISTRŪ (Jacques Cujas et al. eds., Lyon, Franc. le Preux 1593).

p. 12 – GILES JACOB, EVERY MAN HIS OWN LAWYER: OR, A SUMMARY OF THE LAWS OF ENGLAND (New York, Hugh Gaine 1768).

p. 13 – THE POCKET COMPANION; OR, EVERY MAN HIS OWN LAWYER (Philadelphia, S. Parmele 1818).

p. 14 – WILLIAM JONES, AN ESSAY ON THE LAW OF BAILMENTS (John Balmanno ed., Brattleboro, William Fessenden 1813).

pp. 15 & 25 – HILARY DOUGLAS C. PEPLAR, THE LAW THE LAWYERS KNOW ABOUT (1923).

p. 16 – CLARENCE DARROW, THE FAMOUS EXAMINATION OF BRYAN AT THE SCOPES EVOLUTION TRIAL (Little Blue Book No. 1424) (1929).

www.ingramcontent.com/pod-product-compliance
Lightning Source LLC
Chambersburg PA
CBHW022344280326
41934CB00006B/768